> We hold these truths to be self-evident, that all men are created equal, that they are endowed by their Creator with certain unalienable Rights, that among these are Life, Liberty and the pursuit of Happiness.
>
> —Declaration of Independence
> United States of America[1]

The first document founding the United States of America articulates with profound clarity the fundamental rights of its citizens. Life is listed as the first right. As with liberty and the pursuit of happiness, the right to life has been cherished by Americans since our humble beginnings, and our nation continues to promote these rights around the world with the firm conviction that they encompass the universal values inherent to democracy. In the National Security Strategy (NSS), President Obama continues this tradition of projecting American values, emphasizing that fundamental to American leadership is the promotion of universal rights: "…we will advocate for and advance the basic rights upon which our Nation was founded…"[2] Further, the most effective way to promote these values is for the American people to live them and set the moral example.[3]

The NSS emphasizes that our strategic approach to world leadership is cultivated by our sources of strength and influence, including moral leadership.[4] This moral leadership includes the successful promotion of our values and our long-term security is dependent on this success.[5] Indeed, "time and again, our values have been our best national security asset…."[6] Our values also contribute to global security in that, "the United States supports the expansion of democracy and human rights abroad because governments that respect our values are more just, peaceful and legitimate."[7] Yet, our nation will not impose these values; rather the NSS states that "our moral leadership is grounded principally in the power of our example".[8] Successful moral leadership, therefore, requires the use of "soft power"—political power and diplomacy based on attraction and persuasion, rather than on coercion characteristic of "hard power".[9] Arguably, soft power must be credible in order to be effective.[10]

Authentic use of soft power to project American values requires a clear, consistent, and convincing articulation of what those values are, especially when involving basic human rights. However, in recent decades, America has experienced an intense divide regarding the understanding of one of our core values and basic rights— the right to life. The historic Supreme Court decisions legalizing abortion, in essence, removing the right to life for the unborn, have had a polarizing effect on the nation, culminating in the most divisive issue in contemporary America.[11] Gallup research reveals that the nation is equally divided.[12] It also reveals that this division has been consistent and unchanged since the 1973 Supreme Court ruling.[13] The abortion legislation itself acknowledged the severity of this divide and that both sides are strongly opinionated.[14] The Supreme Court Justices were clearly divided on the issue themselves, culminating in a 7-2 ruling.[15] Abortion continues to be a major issue for voters across the full spectrum of politics, from Presidential campaigns, through elections to the House and Senate, and into elections at the state and local level.[16] Averaging an attendance of 250,000 to 400,000 each year, the annual March for Life in Washington D.C. protesting the Supreme Court decisions continues to be the largest and most perpetual protest in our nation's history.[17] Yet this divide is not just a domestic concern. Abortion laws and opinions vary greatly around the world and continue to be a divisive issue within the United Nations, revealing a polarization within the international community as well.[18] The divide over the abortion issue has been so intense and continuous it can properly be called a "wicked problem".[19]

The reason this wicked problem persists is because the logic behind legalized abortion does not appear credible. The Supreme Court decisions that legalized abortion as a private decision of reproductive freedom, simultaneously and consequentially removed the right to life for unborn children (Roe vs. Wade and the companion case heard the same day, Doe vs. Bolton, January 22, 1973).[20] These monumental decisions were a sudden and perplexing reversal of the common law understanding throughout the United States that human life included the unborn and that abortion was legally punishable as a crime.[21] Abortion legislation appears to contradict the "right to life" so powerfully articulated in the Declaration of Independence and reaffirmed in the Constitution.[22] Further, this legislation has generated contradictions within the law itself and is inconsistent with other professions concerning the status of the unborn child.

This paper addresses the concern that current domestic practice and global projection of American values regarding human life are flawed, and do not reflect the intent of our Founding Fathers. The issue of legalized abortion will be examined by asking the question whether or not the unborn child is a human being. This paper will examine a confusing legal dualism resulting from abortion legislation and some difficulties legalized abortion has posed for the Department of Defense. Some of the disturbing consequences of the status quo will be explored, and the paper ends by making the argument that abortion violates the first and most basic of human rights, the right to life. In addition, the conclusion poses a challenge to the national and global conscience. Due to its power and strategic influence, the United States is in a unique position to provide the moral leadership necessary to reexamine the value of human life and provide resolution on a woman's right to abortion versus an unborn child's right to life.

Is the Unborn Child a Human Being?

The humanity of the unborn typically initiates a debate about the rights of the unborn. Often, the argument is made that the question of when life begins cannot be answered, and as a result of this uncertainty, no one knows when life originates or becomes a human being.[23] However, compelling evidence exists within multiple disciplines—science and biology, philosophy, religion, and law—that human life begins at conception. Further, it appears that as intellectual advances continue within these disciplines the reality of the unborn child as a human being only becomes clearer.[24] This growing clarity will continue to intensify and sustain the debate, and contribute to the disputed credibility of our current abortion legislation. Additionally, advances within these disciplines tend to be objective. As a result, they can have a powerful, unifying effect that extends beyond national boundaries, and contributes to a global and universal understanding of values.

Science and Biology

Many within the scientific and biological professions define human life as beginning at conception, and argue the origin of human life is primarily a scientific question.[25] Scientists hold that the determination of when life begins rests solely within their purview and domain, and it is seriously wrong for other disciplines to posture themselves above scientific findings.[26] Science and biology emphasize that conception is the moment when the human DNA is established. At the same time, the chromosomal structure becomes uniquely human and completely distinct from that of the mother and

4

father.[27] Even the sex of the human "zygote", as it is called at this initial stage of development, is determined.[28] This is when the process formally begins and a human being is created—all that is needed and defines a human being is present.[29]

Philosophy

Based on the philosophical principle of non-contradiction, human life begins at conception. According to Aristotle, philosophy deals with the first principles, of which the principle of non-contradiction is the most important foundation.[30] Variations exist, but in essence the principle states that for something to be and not be at the same time is impossible.[31] Aristotle provides this simple foundation as a means for rational thought and the avoidance of error in the establishment of a truth.[32] A bird cannot be a bird and not be a bird at the same time; a tree cannot be a tree and not be a tree; two plus two cannot equal four, and at the same time equal five. The same is true for a human being: the existence of a human being and non-existence of a human being at the same time is impossible. A developing human being is, therefore, still a human being. The early (and later) stages of fetal development do not un-define the status of a human being. Using non-contradiction, the moment of conception is when a new life begins growing and developing "as" a human being, not "into" a human being. Conversely, if life does not begin at conception, non-contradiction concludes that any determination thereafter is relative, subjective, and completely arbitrary.[33] Considering the debate over partial-birth abortion and the current administration's opposition to the ban on the procedure, relative determination has extended throughout pregnancy, up to and including the actual date of birth.[34]

Religion

The majority of Americans claim a Judeo-Christian background and as a result of this religious context, most would answer that the unborn child is a human being.[35] Catholic teaching is clear in this understanding, but some variances exist among Protestant Churches.[36] Historically, religion was very important to the Founding Fathers and led to their deliberate use of the religious phrase "endowed by their Creator" when describing our basic rights in the Declaration of Independence.[37] Aside from the many biblical quotes used by Christians to emphasize life in the womb is a human being, this religious understanding was present at the very founding of our nation.[38] Beyond our Founding Fathers' religious understanding, many other religions around the world believe the unborn child is a human being (e.g. Islam, Hinduism, and Buddhism), adding significance to the impact legalized abortion may have on diplomacy.[39] Considering our involvement in the Middle-East, Islam, for example, is very conservative and opposes abortion in most instances.[40]

Legal Dualism

Perhaps the most unusual development concerning the question of the unborn's humanity is the confusion it has generated within the legal profession itself. Roe vs. Wade answers that the unborn child is a "potential" human being and is not granted the status of a human being as long as he or she remains inside their mother's womb.[41] As a result, in the United States, a woman is free to terminate her pregnancy at any stage of fetal development, although some states restrict late term abortions.[42] Yet within this freedom to choose abortion, confusion exists due to a persistent contradiction that has resulted in legal dualism. Under certain circumstances, the unborn child is not a potential human being, but is granted the legal status of an "actual" human being.

6

Modern advances in fetal care, for example, allow doctors to perform healing procedures in utero, formally treating the unborn fetus as an actual human "patient".[43] Medical negligence on the part of doctors or health care professionals to properly care for the fetus can result in criminal prosecution for the death or injury of an unborn child.[44] Another example of this dualism is when a perpetrator is charged with a double homicide in the murder or accidental killing of a pregnant woman. Scott Peterson, one of the most notorious of these cases, is on death row for a double homicide, the murder of his wife and their unborn child.[45] This case culminated in President George W. Bush signing new federal legislation, "The Unborn Victims of Violence Act of 2004" (also called Laci and Conner's Law), that defines a "child in utero" as "a member of the species *Homo sapiens*, at any stage of development, who is carried in the womb".[46] Further, the law holds that, outside of abortion, "if a person … intentionally kills or attempts to kill the unborn child, that person shall...be punished…for intentionally killing or attempting to kill a human being."[47] The law has some limitations leading to diversity at the state level. Although most states have codified the crime of killing an unborn child (outside the context of induced abortion) as a form of homicide or feticide, many have not.[48] Additionally, this dualism extends into other fields of jurisprudence, culminating in an extraordinary litany of case studies highlighting the confusion this dualism continues to generate.[49]

Currently, the law enjoys a position of dominance in the determination of when life begins. However, in order to be credible, law should reflect consistency, within itself and with other disciplines. Most importantly, the law should be in harmony with our founding values. The presence of legal dualism, inconsistency, and disharmony reveal a serious flaw in our current understanding of the universal value of life and explain the domestic divide on this issue. Legal dualism also raises grave concerns regarding the objectivity, accuracy, and truthfulness of the law. At a minimum, persistent legal dualism combined with the absence of domestic unity clearly expose the national divide on the value of the right to life versus the value of the right to abortion. In addition to the effect on credibility, the projection of legal dualism and the absence of domestic unity will at the same time project confusion regarding America's understanding of the "right to life" from our Declaration of Independence.[50] Confusion also affects credibility and impedes effective values projection, ultimately weakening our use of soft power and moral leadership concerning the core value of life.

Beyond Abortion: Current and Potential Consequences of the Status Quo

Building on the foundation established by initial abortion legislation, additional consequences and new directions continue to develop and unfold. Just as abortion laws created a national divide at their inception, so present is a divide regarding these new developments in abortion law progression.[51] The controversy, confusion, and ethical concerns surrounding these new developments will also impede successful projection of American values, and raise more questions about the credibility of the initial abortion legislation that has led to these new developments.[52] The same controversy and ethical confusion regarding these new developments also exists within the international community, revealing a serious need for clear direction and moral leadership.[53]

Abortion has been part of the American culture for forty years and has received considerable social acceptance as a constitutional right in the exercise of reproductive freedom. The basis and justification for abortion legislation is the Supreme Court

8

defining the unborn as potential human beings. With this foundational definition, a new series of different uses for abortion freedom now exist. New developments in the fields of biology, science, and medicine have discovered that human embryos and fetal tissue can be used for research, experimentation, and patient treatment.[54] Justification for these new fields of study is based on the same premise that justifies abortion—the embryo or the unborn fetus are not a human being, rather the unborn are categorically and legally defined as potential human beings.

Fetal Harvesting

Fetal harvesting is the process of extracting (harvesting) fetal tissue as a byproduct of abortion. Amidst controversy and an earlier prohibition on the practice by President George H. W. Bush, President Clinton lifted the ban in 1993.[55] The law that lifted the ban still prohibits profiting from the practice, but evidence suggests that there are ways for abortion providers and pregnant women to profit financially and not violate the law.[56] Currently, the entire fetus can be harvested for its tissue and organs.[57] Professor Richard Gardner of Oxford University, a renowned expert on human reproduction and an advisor to Britain's Human Fertilization and Embryology Authority, recently raised the prospect of using organs from aborted fetuses for transplantation into adults.[58] He predicts that in the very near future a woman will have the option to carry a pregnancy into the third trimester, have an abortion for the purpose of harvesting the fetal kidneys, and use them for a patient in need of transplant.[59]

Fetal Screening

After conception, diagnostic tests can be performed on the fetus to detect various genetic disorders, and in the case of a positive finding, a woman can elect abortion.[60] As researchers identify more genetic markers and develop blood tests for diseases, concern has arisen over the use of such tests to discriminate and deny people health and life insurance, or future employment. An example is the case when genetic testing reveals a fetus with a serious genetic disorder, one that will require expensive medical treatment, and the woman does not choose abortion.[61] Considering the rising costs of health care and diminishing resources, potential future laws may require fetal screening and may also require abortions when a genetic defect is identified.[62] Moral and ethical questions arise about what constitutes a genetic defect.[63] Down Syndrome is a common example of when abortion is chosen, and has significantly contributed to a reduction in this defect.[64] Disputed examples include mild deformity, moderate and easily treatable disease, addictive drug or alcohol exposure, HIV/AIDS, diagnosable mental disorders, or when the fetus is blind or deaf.

Besides genetic defects, sex selection is another reason for choosing abortion. Sex selection is common practice in countries like China and India, but the United Nations Population Fund and the Council of Europe have also found it to be a disturbing trend in Europe.[65] Population control expert Steve Mosher, president of the Population Research Institute, has discovered sex selection is also a growing practice in the United States.[66] Additional ethical and sociological questions arise given the practice consistently discriminates, favoring selection of a male over a female, significantly impacting historically natural ratios.[67]

Embryonic Experimentation and Research

Another form of harvesting occurs with the extraction of stem cells from human embryos. The popularity of these particular cells is that they can develop into different cell types and may offer a renewable source of replacement cells to treat diseases, conditions, and disabilities.[68] Although earlier legislation under the George W. Bush

Administration restricted this practice, current legislation under the Obama Administration lifted restrictions in support of this research.[69] Unlike fetal harvesting that occurs immediately after abortion when the fetus is not alive, the ethical concern here is that a living human embryo is destroyed in this process.[70]

Embryonic research, however, extends far beyond treating patients. A host of new fields of scientific advancement are emerging and raise more ethical questions as the wicked problem continues to grow. Just as with the fetus, genetic screening is possible at the embryonic stage of development, as is sex selection, which is openly advertised by companies offering in-vitro services.[71] This practice avoids abortion altogether by not following through with embryo implantation after in-vitro fertilization.[72] However, this research is very powerful in that it opens new doors with its eugenics implications.[73] In the future, genetic bioengineering of human beings through in-vitro fertilization, embryo selection, and embryo manipulation, will be able to produce genetically enhanced people who are not only devoid of genetic defects, but are modified to be stronger, smarter, and live longer.[74]

This future may potentially require genetic bioengineering in order to avoid the financial and social strain of genetic defects, illness, and disease. China, for example, continues to advance genetic bioengineering in this direction, believing discoveries that significantly benefit society should be exploited to the full degree possible.[75] This research has also introduced cloning and a host of possibilities as this capability is refined for human purposes.[76] As with all of these new developments, ethical concerns abound regarding human cloning as well.[77] Finally, biotechnical use of embryos for genetic engineering allows for the creation of completely new species through the combination of human and animal DNA.[78] This research can provide advancements in treating and understanding various kinds of human illness and disease.[79] As human-animal experiments continue, and if these new species are allowed to mature, uncertainty will exist regarding their moral status. Depending on the animal and human combination of DNA, complexity is real and with the entanglement, a debate will form concerning the value and right of this complex DNA fusion.[80]

Trends and Exploitation of the Poor

Current domestic legislation still places some restrictions on fetal harvesting and embryonic experimentation, but the pattern of removing these restrictions by successive administrations continues to occur over time.[81] Recently, under the current administration, the Supreme Court ruled that federal funding can now be used to support embryonic stem cell research.[82] Further, restrictive legislation will be difficult to sustain because abortion has been firmly established as a constitutional right, protected by privacy, and an embryo or fetus is defined as a potential (rather than an actual) human being. The pattern of decreased restrictions in fetal and embryonic research by successive administrations indicates that those who defend abortion rights will work with the same dedication to defend these new developments. The American Civil Liberties Union (ACLU), for example, strongly opposes fetal rights legislation and believes this legislation threatens a women's right to abortion.[83] International practices and restrictions regarding fetal and embryo research vary greatly by country, and continue to evolve.[84] Some countries such as Ireland, Italy, Germany, Norway, and Argentina are restrictive; others such as China, Singapore, India and Japan are liberal.[85] Of concern is the reality that few restrictions exist to prevent reckless and unethical acceleration of fetal and embryo research. This acceleration may yield high profits, and could

12

potentially lead to a human cloning/human organ black market and involvement by organized crime.[86]

A significant ethical factor to consider regarding the new developments in fetal and embryo research is the exploitation of poor women, especially in developing countries.[87] Rather than paying for an abortion, a woman could sell her fetus to companies involved with fetal harvesting.[88] Income from these sales could be profitable, culminating in a reverse prostitution; a woman sells her body for pregnancy rather than for sex. Further, as refinements in early pregnancy tests and abortifacient drug products such as the "after-morning pill" continue to be made, abortion may be chosen more often for the purpose of income. Since the 1980's, women have already been able to sell their eggs in support of embryo research and in-vitro services. A woman can earn as much as $30,000 to support her family.[89]

Although abortion was legalized to support reproductive freedom, abortion has expanded to justify additional and perplexing experimentation and research, raising an endless stream of ethical and legal questions which impact the universal value of life. As a consequence of the status quo, we now live in the age of fetal harvesting, fetal screening, genetic fetal selection, fetal sex selection, embryo screening, genetic embryo selection, embryo sex selection, embryo genetic engineering, embryo experimentation, cloning, and human-animal genetic splicing. The new developments continue to generate more controversy and turmoil in the United States and within the international community. For example, in 2005 the United Nations passed a resolution that banned human cloning.[90] The American Society for Cell Biology strongly opposed the ban, stressing the importance of cloning research for medical and therapeutic purposes.[91] In

2008, the United Nations stated that the cloning ban needed to be reassessed.[92] The largest public policy women's organization in the United States, Concerned Women for America, opposed the reassessment, and claims that human cloning will exploit women because massive numbers of women's eggs would be needed to produce clone stem cells.[93] Without moral leadership, disparate policy and practices over these new developments will likely continue, and ultimately prevent consistent values projection regarding the value and definition of human life.

Impact on the Department of Defense

Inconsistent policy and practices concerning the unborn extend to our military personnel, inhibiting their role in diplomacy and values projection. Chief of Staff of the Army General Ray Odierno recently emphasized the diplomatic role every soldier plays in representing our values and our country. "They represent us; they represent our country—the moral and ethical values that they bring forward, they represent America."[94] Policy inconsistencies for the Department of Defense (DOD) center on the constitutionality of restricting abortion for military personnel. The DOD abides by the laws of host countries, making it especially difficult for female service members and their dependents to have an abortion while stationed in countries that restrict abortion or where it is illegal.[95] Countries such as Korea, Afghanistan, and Djibouti ban abortion with the exception of the life of the mother, while Bahrain and the Netherlands allow for unrestricted abortion.[96] In addition, Turkey, Portugal, Italy, Spain and Germany allow for abortion, but restrict it to the first trimester.[97]

Since abortion was legalized in 1973, DOD legislation dealing with the issue has experienced an odyssey of changes and varying interpretations used to allow or deny abortion services.[98] Federal funding for abortion has historically been restricted on military installations to women and their dependents.[99] Recently, however, the National Defense Authorization Act for FY 2013 partially loosened these restrictions. For instance, federal funds via military health care can now be used for abortions in cases of rape, incest, or when the life of the mother would be at risk if the fetus was carried to term.[100] Although the FY 2013 change expands coverage for abortions, the DOD is not in alignment with civilian availability, and therefore, the legality of the restrictions remains in question.[101]

Compounding the complexity of the practice of abortion for military personnel is access and the reluctance of physicians to perform the procedure. Military physicians tend to be conservative on social issues. Many will not perform abortions for reasons of conscience, so even if restrictions were completely lifted, a general unwillingness by health care personnel in uniform to perform the procedure already exists.[102] The alternative, contracting foreign physicians, creates even more problems. Many foreign doctors are not trained to the same standards as the U.S. military physicians. Depending on the country, foreign physicians may have a conscience objection to performing abortions, making a willing physician even more difficult to acquire.[103] Due to the DOD practice of respecting host nation laws, a local physician is not an option in countries like Korea, Afghanistan, and Djibouti where abortion is illegal.[104]

As new developments in human fetal and embryo research and experimentation continue to evolve and become more prevalent, conscience issues can expand beyond health care personnel. Service members not only contribute to the projection of American values, they are also required to defend them. Questioning the morality of these new developments and their acceptance as part of American values, individual

15

service members may also experience a struggle of conscience. As a result, the individual service member's role in diplomacy may be reduced, and a division over the value of human life versus reproductive freedom is apparent. Effective values projection requires consistency and, currently, the policies and practices concerning the unborn are disparate. Conflicting values are promoted instead, detracting from the integrity of our values projection objectives.

Courses of Action/Recommendation

Recommendations on how to resolve this wicked problem are threefold and are based on the status of the unborn child. First, the unborn child's status as a human being is relative. Second, the unborn child is not a human being. Third, the unborn child is a human being. The last two courses of action are more proactive and strive for resolution. One moves in the direction of abortion as the basic right, the other returns to life as the basic right and extends existence to the unborn child. Both assess the environment and create a vision, arguably the most important task required of strategic leaders providing moral leadership.[105]

The Unborn Child's Status as a Human Being is Relative

This course of action is the current one and holds for the status quo. This course of action warrants no change, and accepts dualism and confusion as part of our human condition. This approach allows our universal values and projection of soft power to continue to be in conflict. The gaps are evident by the varied policy proposals of our elected senior officials, our domestic division, and the divide within multiple disciplines. This course of action offers no solution to the pending legal and ethical dilemmas created by new developments and research. The status quo is complacent in acknowledging problems and failing to propose or act on solutions, which in turn impedes effective and consistent values projection.

Historically, the United States has been unsettled with moral relativism regarding democratic values. Slavery was originally part of the American culture, but over time our nation recognized that slavery was incompatible with the democratic values upon which our nation was founded, and the country was willing to fight a civil war to bring about necessary change. The Suffrage Movement is another example that reveals American discontent with moral relativism. As a result of the Suffrage Movement, women now have the right to vote and run for public office when prior to this movement women were denied these rights. The Civil War and the Suffrage Movement are just two examples where action was required to bring about democratic growth and necessary change. History reveals that as democracy progresses, nations that embrace democracy experience growing pains. Moral relativism and our current status quo stifle this necessary growth and ultimately prevent the maturation of democratic values.

The Unborn Child is not a Human Being, A Value of Abortion and Beyond

Using the Roe vs. Wade ruling as a foundation, proponents of this course of action sustain the definition of the unborn child as a potential human being. From this perspective, this course of action supports unrestricted abortion throughout all stages of pregnancy and goes beyond initial abortion legislation to support developments in fetal and embryo usage and research. In an effort to firmly establish abortion as an enduring value of American culture and reinforce Roe vs. Wade and Doe vs. Bolton, proponents have introduced new legislation, the Freedom of Choice Act (FOCA).[106] This bill proposes that women have the fundamental right to choose to bear a child, terminate a pregnancy prior to fetal viability, or terminate a pregnancy after fetal viability to protect the life or health of the woman.[107] Health includes the holistic, full-spectrum of health as articulated in Doe vs. Bolton.[108] Advocates support the removal of all abortion restrictions, and as a result, support the reversal of the current partial-birth abortion ban.[109] Proponents for this option also oppose fetal rights legislation and argue that granting rights to the fetus threatens legalized abortion.[110] In light of this, supporters call for the reversal of the Unborn Victims of Violence Act (Laci and Conner's Law) because this law endows the fetus with legal rights separate from the expectant mother.[111] Continuing in this direction, advocates support fetal harvesting and experimentation.[112] Maintaining consistency, live human embryos are also categorized as potential human beings. Therefore, this option supports the research, experimentation, and stem cell harvesting from living human embryos.[113]

This approach recognizes that if life begins at conception, the result is an immediate state of massive contradiction.[114] In an effort to provide moral leadership and remove existing contradiction, this course of action strives to resolve legal dualism with legal consistency. By maintaining consistency with the initial abortion legislation and following that legislation to its logical developments, proponents support modern fetal and embryo usage and research.[115] If the fetus can be aborted and stem cells can be harvested from living human embryos, legal consistency cannot logically object to any form of fetal or embryo experimentation or research, especially if the motivation is the advancement of human medicine and patient treatment.[116]

Focusing on the legal perspective alone, this option remains in conflict with the scientific community, and does not align with philosophy, religion, or the historical understanding of life articulated in the Declaration of Independence and reaffirmed in

18

the Constitution.[117] Further, this course of action does not set a good moral example for the world. Countries such as Germany, recall the Nuremberg trials of Nazi doctors who performed human experiments on concentration camp prisoners, wisely recognize a need for oversight of medical experiments involving human subjects.[118] Considering their historical experience, Germany strictly prohibits embryo research.[119] Finally, proponents for this legal consistency avoid the many ethical concerns surrounding the life or health of the fetus or embryo that have come about as a result of modern advances in fetal and embryo research and usage. This approach does not provide a solution consistent with the historical American value of life and fails to provide resolution for the international community.

The Unborn Child is a Human Being, the New American Value of Life

This course of action or option is a rigorous renewed appreciation for the Founding Fathers value of life as the first right and extends the right to life to the unborn. Recognizing the primacy of science and the importance of consistency with other disciplines—philosophy, religion, and elements of law—this course of action formally defines the embryo or fetus as an actual human being, rather than a potential human being, entitled to a constitutional right to life from the moment of conception. This course of action acknowledges that current laws have created a state of contradiction. Proponents for this option favor the reversal of Roe vs. Wade and Doe vs. Bolton and propose abortion as a punishable crime. Only when the life of the mother is objectively at risk and medically verifiable, with a strict standard of criteria, is abortion allowed in this course of action. The Catholic use of the moral principle of double effect provides sound guidance in the application of this exception clause, articulating cases when abortion is permissible and the logic that justifies the decision to proceed.[120]

19

This course of action provides the moral leadership needed to remove current inconsistent policies and practices concerning the value of life. By re-emphasizing life as a core democratic value and basic human right, this approach also sets the moral example for the world. Losing sight of this value as a fundamental democratic right has resulted in the growing confusion and dualism, and is currently used to justify a host of new procedures, such as human fetal harvesting, embryo experimentation, and cloning. A reversal of such practices is needed in order for our nation to be consistent in the projection of the universal value of life, and establish the credibility needed for effective use of soft power in this effort.

Recommendation

The new American value of life that recognizes the unborn child as a human being is the recommended course of action. This option removes the flawed current domestic practice and global projection of American values regarding human life. America's power and influence are still a major force in the modern world, and as a result, nations often look to the United States for moral leadership as well as our democratic values to resolve moral dilemmas. Projection of the new American value of human life responds to this need for moral leadership and sets the moral example to resolve abortion's legal dualism, and the progression of abortion legislation that has resulted in the many ethical dilemmas in fetal and embryonic research.

Forty years of legalized abortion has established reproductive freedom as part of the national culture. Change is never easy in situations like this, but the consequences arising as a result of new developments such as fetal harvesting, fetal screening, genetic fetal selection, fetal sex selection, embryo screening, genetic embryo selection, embryo sex selection, embryo genetic engineering, embryo experimentation, cloning, and human-animal genetic splicing, may challenge even the staunchest of abortion supporters. This recommended option recognizes that our nation is at a crossroads, particularly in light of these new developments. This course of action also acknowledges that current abortion policy and practice is flawed, and has resulted in the current state of legal dualism and ethical confusion, and has been used to support new developments in fetal and embryo usage and research.

Our nation has experienced flawed policy in the past. Leading up to the Civil War, our nation was at a crossroads regarding the status of legalized slavery, as those laws also challenged the national conscience regarding our founding values of equality and the dignity of human life. The infamous Dred Scott Supreme Court decision declared that slaves were the legal property of their owners; that slaves were not citizens and that slaves were not entitled to rights.[121] Change was not easy then, nor will it be easy now, but in the end, moral courage and moral leadership prevailed. In contrast to FOCA, Human Life Amendments have been introduced in an effort to initiate change and implement this course of action.[122] The only formal vote in the Senate on a Human Life Amendment occurred in 1983 with the Hatch-Eagleton Human Life Federalism Amendment.[123] The amendment was an attempt to reverse Roe vs. Wade, but did not receive sufficient votes to pass.[124]

Conclusion: A New Era of Life

Doctor Martin Luther King, Jr., spoke of a dream in our national heritage, a dream established by our Founding Fathers and echoed by Abraham Lincoln: "that all men are created equal...."[125] We now live in the final era of that dream of equality. In order for it to be fully actualized, there is still one last segment of our society that must be granted equality. Currently, the unborn child remains the victim of discrimination, not

21

because of the color of their skin, but because of their location in the womb. As a result, the unborn child is not granted the equality upon which our nation was founded. Just as slavery denied a segment of our society rights, abortion denies the unborn child the first and most basic right, the right to life. Their existence can be terminated at will and with an ever increasing removal of restrictions. Additionally, with modern developments and scientific advancements, aborted fetuses can be used for tissue and organ harvesting, creating a new and potential exploitation of the poor; with in-vitro fertilization, conception occurs outside the womb in a laboratory and these living human embryos can legally be used for experimentation and research.

In the NSS, President Obama humbly and powerfully acknowledges that our nation's history has had imperfections:

> Moreover, America's influence comes not from perfection, but from our striving to overcome our imperfections. The constant struggle to perfect our union is what makes the American story inspiring. That is why acknowledging our past shortcomings—and highlighting our efforts to remedy them—is a means of promoting our values.[126]

Projection of our values, then, allows for acknowledgement of an error, and the associated values projection to correct that error. As new genetic developments and scientific advancements continue to be made in human fetal and embryo research, the foundation for abortion legislation that denies the unborn the right to life will be pushed to new limits and these decisions will accompany American values projection. The words from the Declaration of Independence describing "life" as a self-evident truth endowed by the Creator, listing "life" as the first unalienable right, and declaring "that all men are created equal", may very well have profound implications beyond what our Founding Fathers initially realized.[127] Perhaps these words are prophetic, for within these words are the means to resolve the most divisive issue in modern history, an

22

issue and its consequences that were not foreseen by our Founding Fathers. Then, as now, our Founding Fathers realized that if we cannot get the first "right" correct, then every other freedom and value that democracy is built on will be relative and subject to future removal.

The United States has a window of opportunity to use these founding words describing truths we hold to be "self-evident", to correct the error that has plagued our nation and the world.[128] In an era of diminishing fiscal resources and reduced military spending, appreciation for the use of soft power as a dominant means of achieving America's value objectives continues to grow.[129] Especially when it involves the promotion of democracy, human rights, and freedom, soft power will often prove more successful than hard power.[130] Our nation must be prepared to exercise the moral courage necessary to accept the associated controversy that will follow this soft power projection of the new American value of life. The reversal of our current law will be unpopular for many, but an equal number will welcome this change. To facilitate success, we must fully exploit the necessary science and appropriate disciplines to defend the new American value of life. Based on the words from our Declaration of Independence and the Constitution, we must press on with a renewed conviction that recognizes the humanity of the unborn at every stage of development. In doing so, we will set a new moral example for the world. Projection of the new American value of human life will ultimately distinguish our nation, renew its legacy, and elevate its moral leadership. Given the historical connection of values with security, the establishment of this new era of life may very well usher in a new and wonderful era of peace.

Endnotes

[1] Founding Fathers of the United States of America, *Declaration of Independence, July 4, 1776* (Washington, D.C.: The Heritage Foundation, 2010), 6.

[2] Barack Obama, *National Security Strategy* (Washington, D.C.: The White House, May 2010), ii, 35.

[3] Ibid., ii, 1, 5, 10, 36.

[4] Ibid., 7.

[5] Ibid., 10, 35, 36.

[6] Ibid., 35.

[7] Ibid., 37.

[8] Ibid., 10, 36.

[9] Joseph S. Nye, Jr., *The Future of Power* (New York: Public Affairs, 2011), 21, 84.

[10] Ibid., 83.

[11] David Crary, "Roe vs. Wade: 40 Years Later, Deep Divide is Legacy," January 22, 2013, http://news.msn.com/us/roe-v-wade-40-years-later-deep-divide-is-legacy/ (accessed February 10, 2013). "Forty years and roughly 55 million abortions later the ruling's legacy is the opposite of consensus. Abortion ranks as one of the most intractably divisive issues in America, and is likely to remain so as rival camps see little space for common ground." "Fetal Rights," *Law Brain*, April 30, 2010, http://lawbrain.com/wiki/Fetal_Rights (accessed January 10, 2013). In the years following Roe vs. Wade, abortion became one of the most contentious issues in U.S. law.

[12] Steven Ertelt, "Gallup Finds Pro-Choice Americans Back Most Abortion Limits," August 8, 2011, http://www.lifenews.com/2011/08/08/gallup-finds-pro-choice-americans-back-most-abortion-limits/ (accessed January 19, 2013). This article reports on the Gallup research that confirms division on the abortion issue; it also reveals that many pro-choice Americans favor abortion limits, and concludes that the overall division between pro-choice and pro-life is an equal 47% divide.

[13] Gallup, "Abortion," February 2013, http://www.gallup.com/poll/1576/Abortion.aspx (accessed February 14, 2013). The latest Gallup poll on the topic shows 52% of Americans saying abortion should be legal under certain circumstances, 25% wanting it legal in all cases and 20% wanting it outlawed in all cases, roughly the same breakdown as in the 1970s.

[14] U.S. Supreme Court, "Roe vs. Wade, 410 U.S. 113 (1973)," January 22, 1973, http://caselaw.lp.findlaw.com/scripts/getcase.pl?court=us&vol=410&invol=113 (accessed November 12, 2012). Part 1, paragraph 2. The Supreme Court acknowledged the intensity of this national divide, "vigorous and opposing views, even among physicians".

[15] Ibid. The division existed within the high court itself. In their dissenting arguments, both Justice White and Justice Rehnquist strongly emphasized that the court had gravely over-extended its authority. The ruling of the court did not have its basis in the Constitution for privacy. Specifically, that this was not a proper application of the 14th Amendment: "To reach its result, the Court necessarily has had to find within the scope of the Fourteenth Amendment a right that was apparently completely unknown to the drafters of the Amendment." Justice Rehnquist further argued that since most states had already established laws restricting abortion only for when the life of the mother was at risk, that the right to an abortion was not the universally accepted opinion of the day. He also accurately predicted that as a result of the Supreme Court's decision, the issue would become more confusing in the future.

[16] H.M. Epstein, "Abortion the Top Issue for Women Voters in Swing States," *Examiner.com*, October 19, 2012, http://www.examiner.com/article/abortion-the-top-issue-for-women-voters-swing-states (accessed February 13, 2013). Gallup reported female registered voters named abortion as the single most important issue for women in this election. Patrick Marley and Lee Bergquist, "Abortion, Birth Control are Wedge Issues in Governor's Race," *Milwaukee Wisconsin Journal Sentinel*, Oct. 2, 2010, http://www.jsonline.com/news/statepolitics/104221094.html (accessed February 11, 2012). There are many election articles across the full spectrum of government consistently highlighting abortion as a voter concern.

[17] Hilary White, "Some March for Life Fun Facts and a Few Thoughts on Media Blackouts," January 28, 2011, http://www.lifesitenews.com/news/some-march-for-life-fun-facts-and-a-few-thoughts-on-media-blackouts (accessed December 22, 2012). The March for Life in Washington is by far the largest single annual political event in the United States, and possibly in the western world. "March for Life," January 28, 2013, http://www.conservapedia.com/March_for_Life (accessed February 11, 2013). The March for Life is the largest and longest annual gathering in the history of the United States. About 400,000 (and growing) gather annually in Washington, D.C. By comparison, the biggest sports events attract attendance of only 100,000-250,000, and the biggest cities can accommodate tourism of only about 200,000 at any particular time.

[18] Bethany Monk, "UN Pushes Abortion as Human Right", October 8, 2012, http://www.citizenlink.com/2012/10/08/un-pushes-abortion-as-human-right/ (accessed February 12, 2013). The United Nations Human Rights Council recently passed a resolution endorsing guidelines supporting abortion as a basic human right. Twenty of the 47 council members opposed the resolution and submitted an opposition letter. The resolution was ultimately adopted without a vote. Center for Reproductive Rights, "The World's Abortion Laws 2012," http://www.worldabortionlaws.com/map/ (accessed February 6, 2013).

[19] Stephen J. Gerras, ed., *Strategic Leadership Primer, 3rd Edition* (Carlisle Barracks, Pennsylvania: US Army War College, 2010), 36. Problems that do not have easy solutions are popularly referred to as "wicked problems".

[20] United States Conference of Catholic Bishops (USCCB), "Summary of Roe vs. Wade and Other Key Abortion Cases," http://old.usccb.org/prolife/issues/abortion/roevwade/CaseSummariesforwebsite4-18.pdf (accessed December 15, 2012). The Supreme Court ruled that the abortion decision is protected under the 9th and 14th Amendments as a constitutional right to privacy; that a fetus is a potential life and therefore does not possess constitutional rights of its own. Ibid., "Fetal Rights,"

Law Brain. In making its decision, the Court ruled that a fetus is not a person under the terms of the Fourteenth Amendment to the U.S. Constitution. Ibid., U.S. Supreme Court, "Roe vs. Wade," Preface, Conclusion. The Conclusion states that Doe vs. Bolton is to be read together with the Roe vs. Wade ruling.

[21] James S. Cole, "Abortion Law Before Roe vs. Wade," http://www.missourilife.org/law/preroe.htm (accessed December 15, 2012). Historically, common law held that abortion was a crime. This understanding was held throughout most of the United States prior to 1973. Although a loosening of the abortion restrictions was on the rise at the state level beginning around 1960, most still held that abortion was a crime unless the life of the mother was at risk. Jone Johnson Lewis, "Abortion History: A Brief History of Abortion in the United States," http://womenshistory.about.com/od/abortionuslegal/a/abortion.htm (accessed 19 December 2012). By 1965, all fifty states banned abortion, with some exceptions which varied by state to save the life of the mother, or in cases of rape, incest, or if the fetus was deformed.

[22] Ibid., *Declaration of Independence*. U.S. Constitution, 14th Amendment. In part, "...nor shall any state deprive any person of life...nor deny to any person...equal protection of the laws."

[23] Steve Wagner, "No One Knows When Life Begins," 2007, http://www.str.org/site/DocServer/3No_one_knows-v3.pdf?docID=139 (accessed December 28, 2012).

[24] Bernard Nathanson, "The Silent Scream," 1984, *You Tube*, video file. http://www.bing.com/videos/search?q=youtube+silent+scream&mid=0B151CCE79CB1AAA519 E0B151CCE79CB1AAA519E&view=detail&FORM=VIRE7 (accessed January 10, 2013). In addition to the graphic visual clarity seen on this ultrasound video of an abortion, Dr. Nathanson discusses a series of remarkable advances in science, medicine, and technology that contribute to an ever increasing understanding of the unborn child as a human being.

[25] "When Does Human Life Begin? Doctors Testify to U.S. Senate," April 23, 1981, http://www.prolife.com/FETALDEV.html (accessed December 22, 2012). Many internationally known geneticists and biologists have testified that human life begins at conception. Keith L. Moore, *The Developing Human, Clinically Oriented Embryology, 6th Edition* (Philadelphia: Saunders, 1998), 2, 18. This standard medical textbook states that "a zygote is the beginning of a new human being ...." and that "Human development begins at fertilization...." Association of Pro-Life Physicians, "When does Human Life Begin?", http://prolifephysicians.org/lifebegins.htm (accessed February 16, 2013). "There is a tremendous consensus in the scientific community about when life begins. Life begins at fertilization, when a sperm unites with an oocyte. Even before the mother is aware that she is pregnant, a distinct, unique life has begun his or her existence inside her. As early as 21 days after conception, the baby's heart has begun to beat his or her own unique blood-type, often different than the mother's. At 40 days after conception, brain waves can be read on an EEG, or an electroencephalogram." Dianne N. Irving, "American Bioethics Advisory Commission: When do Human Beings Begin? Scientific Myths and Scientific Facts," 1999, http://www.all.org/abac/dni003.htm (accessed December 21, 2012). Dr. Irving argues the question as to when a human being begins is strictly a scientific question.

[26] Ibid., Irving, "When do Human Beings Begin?"

[27] Ibid.

[28] Ibid. See Fact #5: "The immediate product of fertilization is genetically already a girl or a boy."

[29] Ibid. "A human being is the immediate product of fertilization. As such he/she is a single-cell embryonic zygote, an organism with 46 chromosomes, the number required of a member of the human species. This human being immediately produces specifically human proteins and enzymes, directs his/her own further growth and development as human, and is a new, genetically unique, newly existing, live human individual. After fertilization the single-cell human embryo doesn't become another kind of thing. It simply divides and grows bigger and bigger, developing through several stages as an embryo."

[30] Gottlieb, Paula, "Aristotle on Non-contradiction," *The Stanford Encyclopedia of Philosophy,* Summer 2011, http://plato.stanford.edu/entries/aristotle-noncontradiction/ (accessed December 13, 2012).

[31] Ibid.

[32] Ibid. According to Aristotle, the principle of non-contradiction is the firmest principle of scientific inquiry, reasoning, and communication; a principle that we cannot do without.

[33] Ibid. See fourth paragraph in Part V. Aristotle holds that opponents of non-contradiction live in a world in which accidents can be linked up in any way they like. Anything goes in such a world, or nothing goes, depending on taste.

[34] Frank Pavone, "Partial Birth Abortion," http://www.priestsforlife.org/partialbirth.html (accessed January 4, 2013). The partial birth abortion procedure is currently illegal. Under the George W. Bush Administration, the Supreme Court upheld the ban in 2007. However, the issue is still hotly contested and the current administration has pledged to reexamine the issue. Michael Gerson, "Obama's Abortion Extremism," *The Washington Post*, April 2, 2008, http://articles.washingtonpost.com/2008-04-02/opinions/36923530_1_abortion-rights-partial-birth-democratic-party (accessed February 3, 2013). President Obama opposed the ban on partial-birth abortion and strongly criticized the Supreme Court decision upholding the partial-birth abortion ban. "Partial-Birth Abortion," http://www.abortionfacts.com/literature/partial-birth-abortion (accessed December 22, 2012). Contrary to claims that the partial birth abortion procedure was rare, prior to the Supreme Court ban on the procedure, one abortion provider openly admitted to performing over 2000 partial birth abortions.

[35] Gallup, "In the US, 77% Identify as Christian," December 24, 2012, http://www.gallup.com/poll/159548/identify-christian.aspx (accessed February 15, 2013). Gallup, "More Americans Pro-Life than Pro-Choice for First Time," May 15, 2009, http://www.gallup.com/poll/118399/More-Americans-Pro-Life-Than-Pro-Choice-First-Time.aspx (accessed February 15, 2013). Gallup breaks down the question into four categories. However, only a consistent minority of have held for unrestricted abortion, 22% in 2009. That same year, 59% of Christians claimed to be pro-life rather than pro-choice.

[36] The Vatican, *Catechism of the Catholic Church, Second Edition* (New York: Doubleday, 1997), 606-608. Mark Tooley, "Protestants and Abortion," January 31, 2013,

http://spectator.org/archives/2013/01/31/protestants-and-abortion (accessed February 10, 2013).

[37] Ibid., *Declaration of Independence*.

[38] Frank A. Pavone, "The Bible's Teaching Against Abortion," http://www.priestsforlife.org/brochures/thebible.html (accessed February 11, 2013). Among the most commonly used: Old Testament: You knit me together in my mother's womb, Psalm 139:13; New Testament: The infant in my womb leapt for joy, Luke 1:44.

[39] "World Religions on Abortion," July 13, 2005, http://www.freerepublic.com/focus/f-news/1442381/posts (accessed February 7, 2013).

[40] Jonathan E. Brockopp, *Islamic Ethics of Life, Abortion, War, and Euthanasia*, (South Carolina: University of South Carolina Press, 2003), 76. The majority of Muslim scholars discourage or prohibit abortion before 120 days and definitely after 120 days as the taking of a life or potential life.

[41] Ibid., U.S. Supreme Court, "Roe vs. Wade". The specific phrase used in Roe vs. Wade when making reference to a pregnant woman's unborn child is "the potentiality of human life".

[42] Ibid., USCCB, "Summary of Roe vs. Wade and Other Key Abortion Cases". In Doe vs. Bolton the Supreme Court health exception expanded the right to abortion for any reason through all three trimesters of pregnancy. U.S. Supreme Court, "Doe vs. Bolton, 410 U.S. 179," January 22, 1973, http://www.priestsforlife.org/government/supremecourt/7301doevbolton.htm (accessed November 4, 2012). Part V. Jodi Jacobson, "Late-term Abortions: Facts, Stories, and Ways to Help," http://www.rhrealitycheck.org/blog/2009/06/02/thirdtrimester-abortions-facts-stories-and-how-you-can-help-0 June 2, 2009, (accessed December 22, 2012). "Late Term Abortion Laws," 2010, http://www.abortionabout.com/latetermabortionlaws.html (accessed February 24, 2013). As of April 2007, 36 states had bans or restrictions on late-term abortions.

[43] Shelly P. Springer, MD, "Prenatal Diagnosis and Fetal Therapy, Fetus as a Patient," February 15, 2012, http://emedicine.medscape.com/article/936318-overview (accessed December 29, 2012). Only in the past few decades has the fetus been considered a patient and become the subject of extensive scientific study and attempts at treatment. Ibid., "Fetal Rights," *Law Brain*. Ibid., Association of Pro-Life Physicians, "When does Life Begin?" This article mentions surgery performed on a 21 week-old fetus in utero for spina-bifida, and "draws attention to the obvious fact that the surgeon is performing surgery on one living human being who is residing in the womb of another living human being."

[44] J. Hernandez, "Doctor Sued For Malpractice For Failure to Monitor Fetal Vital Signs Properly," November 11, 2010, http://www.articlesbase.com/law-articles/doctor-sued-for-malpractice-for-failure-to-monitor-fetal-vital-signs-properly-3647553.html (accessed December 31, 2012). J. Hernandez, "(Unborn) Child dies when Premature Membrane Overlooked by Doctor," December 17, 2010, http://www.articlesbase.com/law-articles/child-dies-when-premature-membrane-rupture-overlooked-by-doctor-3863931.html (accessed December 17, 2012). The lawsuit against the doctor in this case was also successful. Many other articles provide examples to confirm that medical personnel can be held liable in the death or injury of an unborn child.

[45] Charles Montaldo, "Scott Peterson Guilty of First Degree Murder," March, 2005, http://crime.about.com/od/news/a/scott_peterson.htm (accessed November 23, 2012).

[46] *Unborn Victims of Violence Act of 2004 (Laci and Conner's Law),* 108th Congress, 2nd Session (April 1, 2004), Section 1841. http://news.findlaw.com/hdocs/docs/abortion/unbornbill32504.html (accessed January 2, 2013).

[47] Ibid.

[48] National Conference of State Legislators, "Fetal Homicide State Laws," February 2013, http://www.ncsl.org/issues-research/health/fetal-homicide-state-laws.aspx (accessed February 4, 2013). Currently, at least 38 states have fetal homicide laws.

[49] Thomas W. Strahan, "Legal Protection of the Unborn Child Outside the Context of Induced Abortion," *Association for Interdisciplinary Research in Values and Social Change, Vol. 11 No. 1,* March/April 1997, http://www.lifeissues.net/writers/air/air_vol11no1_1997.html (accessed November 29, 2012). This article lists a number of complicated case studies, highlighting the confusion that exists within the legal community. Ibid., "Fetal Rights," *Law Brain.* This article provides an additional series of legal concerns; highlighting that states exhibit a wide variety of approaches to fetal rights, and accentuating the existence of an incoherent approach to legal claims regarding the rights of the fetus and the sometimes competing rights of the woman.

[50] Ibid., *Declaration of Independence.*

[51] Janet Gallagher, "What's Wrong with Fetal Rights?" *American Civil Liberties Union (ACLU),* http://www.aclu.org/reproductive-freedom/whats-wrong-fetal-rights (accessed February 10, 2013). Fetal rights threaten abortion legislation. This article highlights the extension of the legal dualism. If the fetus is granted rights, the door is open to restrict abortion. The ACLU holds that criminal prosecution should occur if the fetus is injured when a woman intends to give birth, yet at the same time a woman must still have the right to choose abortion if she does not want to have the child. Quoted in this article is Ronald Reagan claiming abortion was akin to murder. He once provided a summary of this legal dualism: "Isn't it strange that the same woman could have taken the life of her unborn child and it was abortion, not murder, but if somebody else does it, that's murder?"

[52] Christopher Kaczor, "Fetal Research and Consent," 2009, http://www.lifeissues.net/writers/kac/kac_11fetalresearch.html (accessed January 12, 2013). Research on human fetal life involves numerous complex medical, moral, and legal aspects.

[53] Kristina Hug, "Embryonic Stem Cell Research: An Ethical Dilemma," March 23, 2011, http://www.eurostemcell.org/factsheet/embryonic-stem-cell-research-ethical-dilemma (accessed February 1, 2013). Embryonic stem cells offer hope for new therapies, but their use in research has been hotly debated. (In Europe,) different countries have chosen to regulate embryonic stem cell research in very different ways.

[54] "Fetal Tissue Research," *Law Brain,* December 2, 2009, http://lawbrain.com/wiki/Fetal_Tissue_Research (accessed February 4, 2013). Research on fetal tissue led to significant advances in the scientific understanding of fetal development and in the diagnosis and treatment of fetal diseases and defects. It also played a role in advancing the

scientific understanding of cancer, immunology, and transplantation. National Institute of Health (NIH), "The Promise of Stem Cells," September 2, 2011, http://stemcells.nih.gov/Pages/Default.aspx (accessed January 18, 2013).

[55] Karen Tumuly and Marlene Cimons, "Clinton Lifts Restrictions on Abortion: Health: President Ends Ban on Fetal Tissue Research," *Los Angeles Times*, January 23, 1993, http://articles.latimes.com/1993-01-23/news/mn-1468_1_fetal-tissue-research/2 (accessed February 12, 2013).

[56] Kelly Patricia O'Meara, "Harvesting Fetal Body Parts," 1999, http://www.nrlc.org/Baby_Parts/omeara.html (accessed December 26, 2012). The sale of human tissue or body parts is prohibited by federal law, but traffickers have worked out an arrangement to expedite the process from which they all benefit and still remain within current interpretations of the law. Mona Charen, "Body Parts for Sale, Fetal Harvesting," November 9, 1999, http://www.prolife.com/HarvestingAbortedBabies.html (accessed December 29, 2012).

[57] "Fetal Tissue Research," *Wert's Encyclopedia of American Law*, 2005, http://www.encyclopedia.com/doc/1G2-3437701805.html (accessed February 13, 2013). The National Institutes of Health (NIH) Revitalization Act of 1993 permits the tissue from any type of abortion to be used for fetal tissue research.

[58] Jacob M. Appel, "Are We Ready for a Market in Fetal Organs?" *The Huffington Post*, March 17, 2009, http://www.huffingtonpost.com/jacob-m-appel/are-we-ready-for-a-market_b_175900.html (accessed November 28, 2012). Dr. Richard Gardner believes that the prospect of fetal-adult organ transplantation is a realistic near-term possibility.

[59] Ibid. Scientific research is also underway to produce artificial wombs. This would eliminate abortion as a means to harvest the fetus. It would also eliminate the need for a woman to carry the child, essentially eliminating pregnancy. Likewise an artificial womb creates the possibility of men raising fetuses in their abdomens. If successful, this research may make possible farms of artificial wombs breeding fetuses, creating an endless supply of fetal organs and tissue for medical treatment, patient care, research and experimentation. An additional ethical concern is that large numbers of live embryos will be needed for experiments in the development of an artificial womb.

[60] G. Evars-Kiebooms, "Genetic Screening," *Columbia Encyclopedia*, 1987, http://www.answers.com/topic/genetic-screening (accessed December 29, 2012).

[61] Ibid.

[62] Daniel MacArthur, "Will Prenatal Screening for Serious Diseases Rob Us of Our Creativity?" August 5, 2011, http://www.wired.com/wiredscience/2011/08/what-will-be-the-consequences-of-prenatal-screening-for-serious-diseases (accessed March 7, 2013). "Within the next few years every parent in the industrialized world will be able to make a fully informed decision about whether they wish to have a child who will suffer from a serious, untreatable disease. There will be serious consequences as this technology becomes widely adopted. Parents who choose not to use this technology and have a severely disabled child will likely face social ostracism. As the number of children affected with severe genetic diseases decreases there will likely be decreased funding available for the treatment and care of disease sufferers." Karen Norrgard, "Human Testing, the Eugenics Movement, and IRBs," *Scitable*,

2008, http://www.nature.com/scitable/topicpage/Human-Testing-the-Eugenics-Movement-and-IRBs-724 (accessed February 16, 2013). Many individuals today who support eugenic arguments oppose the decision to knowingly give birth to a child with a genetic disorder, cognitive impairment, or physical disability.

[63] Ibid., Norrgard, "Human Testing, the Eugenics Movement, and IRBs". This article reports on an unusual case where a deaf couple wanted their children to be deaf also, and so deliberately sought out a deaf sperm donor to create embryos that would genetically meet this criteria. They succeeded in their effort, giving birth to two deaf children, but a number of ethical questions remain in the wake of such practices.

[64] Tucker Carlson, "Eugenics American Style," February 21, 2012, http://www.slate.com/articles/news_and_politics/politics/2012/02/rick_santorum_prenatal_testing_and_abortion_tucker_carlson_s_classic_essay_on_prenatal_testing_and_the_abortion_of_down_syndrome_babies_.html (accessed February 14, 2013). "Far more women now are able to detect Down Syndrome pregnancies, and far more end them with abortion." In one study, 88% of those who found they were carrying a child with Down Syndrome aborted the fetus. Other studies have put the rate of Down Syndrome abortions at about 90%, some even higher. The practice of aborting in the case of a Down Syndrome fetus also raises the ethical question about whether prenatal screening is a type of prenatal discrimination against the handicapped.

[65] The Elliot Institute, "Not Just China and India: Sex Selection Abortions Spreading Around the World," January 9, 2013, http://afterabortion.org/2013/not-just-china-and-india-sex-selection-abortions-spreading-around-the-world/ (accessed February 17, 2013). Cultures that favor sons over daughters often pressure or even force women to abort a female fetus against their will. Many fall victim to family violence. Some—in an effort to make them miscarry—have been slapped and shoved around by angry husbands and in-laws, or even kicked in the stomach. Others were denied food, water, and rest, in order to coerce them into aborting the unwanted baby girl.

[66] Ibid. Growing concern over the issue in the United States has resulted in legislation being introduced to Congress to ban sex selection (and race selection) abortions. Given that a woman's constitutional right to abortion is a decision protected by privacy, it seems highly unlikely that any such legislation would ever be passed and would be impossible to enforce even if it was. This concern reveals yet another area of confusion resulting from abortion legislation.

[67] Steven W. Mosher, "Sex Selective Abortions Come Home," National Review, December 6, 2011, http://www.nationalreview.com/corner/284988/sex-selective-abortions-come-home-steven-w-mosher (accessed February 17, 2013). There is clear evidence of sex-selective abortions resulting in a higher ratio of boys to girls than would occur in nature. William Saletan, "Fetal Subtraction, Sex Selection in the United States," Slate, April 3, 2008, http://www.slate.com/articles/health_and_science/human_nature/2008/04/fetal_subtraction.html (accessed February 12, 2013). The 50% increase in male probability is evidence of sex selection, most likely at the prenatal stage.

[68] Ibid., NIH, "The Promise of Stem Cells".

[69] The White House, "Removing Barriers to Responsible Scientific Research Involving Human Stem Cells," March 9, 2009, http://www.whitehouse.gov/the_press_office/Removing-

31

Barriers-to-Responsible-Scientific-Research-Involving-Human-Stem-Cells (accessed February 14, 2013). President Obama issued Executive Order 13505 lifting the earlier restrictions enacted by President Georg W. Bush in his Executive Order 13435, June 20, 2007.

[70] Ibid., Hug, "Embryonic Stem Cell Research: An Ethical Dilemma". Trinity University Center for Bioethics and Human Dignity, "Human Embryonic Stem Cell Research," http://cbhd.org/stem-cell-research/position-statement (accessed February 22, 2013).

[71] American Reproductive Centers, http://www.americanreproductivecenters.com/gender-selection (accessed February 14, 2013). Gender selection is openly advertised as a consideration in the process of in-vitro services.

[72] Seth Adam, "PGD and Sex Selection (Cost and Legality Around the World)," August 5, 2010, http://www.surrogatemother.com/forum/topics/pgd-and-sex-selection-cost-and (accessed February 16, 2013). "The main advantage of Pre-implantation Genetic Diagnosis (PGD) is that it avoids selective pregnancy termination (abortion) as the method and makes it highly likely that the baby will be free of the disease under consideration. PGD requires in-vitro fertilization to obtain embryos for evaluation."

[73] Ibid.

[74] Danielle Simmons, "Genetic Inequality: Human Genetic Engineering," *Scitable*, 2008, http://www.nature.com/scitable/topicpage/Genetic-Inequality-Human-Genetic-Engineering-768 (accessed December 30, 2012). Athletes now and in the future will be able to use this technology to enhance performance in sports, raising a series of new ethical questions regarding genetic doping. Many people fear that pre-implantation genetic diagnosis could technically be applied to select specific non-disease traits (rather than eliminate severe disease, as it is currently used) in implanted embryos, thus amounting to a form of eugenics. Although possible, this genetic technology has not yet been implemented; nonetheless, it continues to bring up many heated ethical issues.

[75] Ibid., Norrgard, "Human Testing, the Eugenics Movement, and IRBs". "Moral values in China are strongly influenced by Marxism. There is a strong ideology that regards each person as a small component of society, as well as widespread sentiment that an individual's interests should be subordinate to the interests of the nation. Therefore, it is not surprising that many Chinese geneticists strive to improve population quality and further eugenic principles. In the West, however, there are still many who support eugenic arguments and oppose the decision to knowingly give birth to a child with a genetic disorder, cognitive impairment, or physical disability, opening the door to designer babies and whether society has a right to choose what types of children are born." Caitlin Chapman, "Fetal Stem Cells in Modern-Day Science," June, 2001, http://www.actionbioscience.org/biotech/chapman.html (accessed February 2, 2013). Stem cell research is one of the new frontiers and scientists should have the opportunity to fully explore it, without restrictions and limitations.

[76] "Human Cloning Foundation," 2012, http://www.humancloning.org (accessed February 17, 2013). The Human Cloning Foundation (HCF) believes that cloning technology can be used to cure diseases and prolong life. The HCF believes that blood can be cloned, organs can be cloned, and that infertility can be cured with the use of this new technology. They are hopeful cloning will help unlock the secrets of cancer and lead to its cure. Further, cloning should lead to advances in cosmetic and plastic surgery, as well as anti-aging therapies and other forms of rejuvenation. Cloning has already revolutionized biology and medicine.

[77] American Medical Association, "Human Cloning," 2013, http://www.ama-assn.org/ama/pub/physician-resources/medical-science/genetics-molecular-medicine/related-policy-topics/stem-cell-research/human-cloning.page (accessed February 17, 2013). Many social, moral, and ethical arguments have been raised in opposition to copying a person.

[78] Paige Comstock, "Ligers, Tigons, and Splice: Human-Animal Hybrids," *Center for Bioethics and Human Dignity*, May 20, 2011, http://cbhd.org/content/ligers-tigons-and-splice-human-animal-hybrids (accessed February 17, 2013).

[79] Ibid.

[80] Ibid.

[81] Ibid., Tumuly and Cimons, "Clinton Lifts Restrictions on Abortion: Health: President Ends Ban on Fetal Tissue Research". Ibid., The White House, "Removing Barriers to Responsible Scientific Research Involving Human Stem Cells".

[82] Meredith Wadman, "Supreme Court Ensures Funding of Research Using Human Embryonic Stem Cells," *Scientific American*, January 7, 2013, http://www.scientificamerican.com/article.cfm?id=supreme-court-ensures-funding-of-research-using-human-embryonic-stem-cells (accessed February 15, 2013).

[83] Ibid., Gallagher, "What's Wrong with Fetal Rights?"

[84] The Witherspoon Council on Ethics and the Integrity of Science, "Overview of International Human Embryonic Stem Cell Laws," *New Atlantis*, Winter 2012, http://www.thenewatlantis.com/publications/appendix-e-overview-of-international-human-embryonic-stem-cell-laws (accessed February 13, 2013).

[85] Lisa M. Krieger, "As the U.S. Hesitates, Other Countries Move Ahead with Embryo Research," May. 06, 2002, http://www.mult-sclerosis.org/news/May2002/OtherCountriesOvertakingUSOnStemCells.html (accessed January 13, 2013).

[86] Kort E. Patterson, "New High Profit Opportunity—Illicit Cloning," 1997, http://www.kortexplores.com/node/123 (accessed March 10, 2013). This article expresses concern that a black market cloning industry will be a lucrative future endeavor that will yield greater returns than the illicit drug trade. Jeneen Interlandi, "Not Just Urban Legend," *Newsweek*, January 9, 2009, http://www.thedailybeast.com/newsweek/2009/01/09/not-just-urban-legend.html (accessed March 9, 2013). Organ trafficking was long considered a myth. But now mounting evidence suggests it is a real and growing problem, even in America.

[87] Ibid., O'Meara, "Harvesting Fetal Body Parts". Ibid., Appel, "Are We Ready for a Market in Fetal Organs". Transforming transplantation into a financial transaction might lead to exploitation of the poor, particularly in developing nations.

[88] Ibid., O'Meara, "Harvesting Fetal Body Parts". Ibid., Appel, "Are We Ready for a Market in Fetal Organs?" This article also argues that a market in fetal organs would empower women to use their reproductive capabilities to their own economic advantage. If a woman has the

fundamental right to terminate a pregnancy, she also has the right to use the products of that terminated pregnancy as she sees fit.

[89] CBS News, "More Women Selling Their Eggs," February 11, 2009, http://www.cbsnews.com/2100-500165_162-4517178.html (accessed February 27, 2013). In this interview, the woman said that the poor economy was the main reason behind her decision to sell her eggs for $7000. One woman earned $30,000 selling her eggs.

[90] The United Nations, "Declaration on Human Cloning," August 3, 2005, http://www.un.org/News/Press/docs/2005/ga10333.doc.htm (accessed February 23, 2013).

[91] The American Society for Cell Biology (ASCB), "Cell Biologist Oppose United Nations Ban on Cloning Research," 2005, http://www.ascb.org/index.php?option=com_content&view=article&id=338%3Acell-biologists-oppose-united-nations-ban-on-cloning-research-&catid=2%3Apolicy&Itemid=31 (accessed February 23, 2013). The cloning issue is easily confused. Two types of human cloning exist. One is for the purpose of creating identical human beings. The ASCB strongly opposes the cloning of human beings. The other involves cloning for medical purposes called therapeutic cloning. The ASCB supports therapeutic cloning. However, therapeutic cloning still requires the destruction of living human embryos.

[92] Libby Greismann, "United Nations Will Reassess Ban On Human Cloning," November 1, 2008, http://lawandbiosciences.wordpress.com/2008/11/01/united-nations-will-reassess-ban-on-human-cloning/ (accessed February 22, 2013).

[93] Wendy Wright, "United Nations Debates Cloning Ban," *Concerned Women for America*, http://www.cwfa.org/articledisplay.asp?id=2582&department=CWA (accessed February 23, 2013).

[94] C. Todd Lopez, "Army Birthday Ball a Celebration of Soldiers and History," June 18, 2012, http://www.army.mil/article/81970/Army_birthday_ball_a_celebration_of_Soldiers_history/ (accessed February 18, 2013).

[95] David F. Burrelli, "Abortion Services and Military Medical Facilities," *Congressional Research Service*, January 9, 2013, http://www.fas.org/sgp/crs/misc/95-387.pdf (accessed February 13, 2013), 9-10. As a result of the "Good Neighbor Policy", the DOD overseas is required to observe local laws, posing problems in countries like Spain, South Korea, and Afghanistan where abortions are very restricted or illegal altogether.

[96] Heather D. Boonstra, "Off Base: The U.S. Military's Ban on Privately Funded Abortions," *Guttmacher Policy Review*, Summer 2010, http://www.guttmacher.org/pubs/gpr/13/3/gpr130302.html (accessed March 6, 2013).

[97] Ibid.

[98] Ibid., Burrelli, "Abortion Services and Military Medical Facilities," i, 1.

[99] Ibid.

[100] Ibid., 1.

[101] Amy E. Crawford, "Under Siege: Freedom of Choice and the Statutory Ban on Abortions on Military Bases," *Chicago Law Review*, Fall 2004, https://litigationessentials.lexisnexis.com/webcd/app?action=DocumentDisplay&crawlid=1&doctype=cite&docid=71+U.+Chi.+L.+Rev.+1549&srctype=smi&srcid=3B15&key=250f657f37522ba8456e3c37b88f9a04 (accessed February 15, 2013).

[102] Ibid., Burrelli, "Abortion Services and Military Medical Facilities," 8.

[103] Ibid., 10.

[104] Ibid., 10. Ibid., Boonstra, "Off Base: The U.S. Military's Ban on Privately Funded Abortions".

[105] Ibid., Gerras, *Strategic Leadership Primer*, 20, 23.

[106] "Freedom of Choice Act, Library of Congress Summary," April 19, 2007, http://www.govtrack.us/congress/bills/110/s1173#summary/libraryofcongress (accessed February 12, 2013).

[107] Ibid. A curious component of FOCA is that the very first part of the bill proposes a law protecting an issue that has never been contested: a woman's right to bear a child. U.S. Law has never interfered with, nor threatened to remove this as a woman's right. More accurately, the bill should be entitled the Freedom of Abortion Act. However, medical and scientific advances in genetics and fetal screening may challenge this right in the future, and may very well be the reason the law has not successfully progressed. In the future, it is possible that women with genetically defective eggs may not be allowed to reproduce unless they do so with a healthy donor egg, and through in-vitro fertilization and implantation. Likewise, men with genetically defective sperm may be prohibited to conceive in order to avoid the continuation of genetic defects.

[108] Ibid., USCCB, "Summary of Roe v. Wade and Other Key Abortion Cases". Ibid., U.S. Supreme Court, "Doe vs. Bolton," Part V. In Doe vs. Bolton, the Supreme Court articulated "health" to be liberally holistic, "all factors—physical, emotional, psychological, familial, and the woman's age—relevant to the well-being of the patient."

[109] Ibid., Gerson, "Obama's Abortion Extremism". President Obama opposed the ban on partial-birth abortion and strongly criticized the Supreme Court decision upholding the partial-birth abortion ban.

[110] Ibid., Gallagher, "What's Wrong with Fetal Rights?" Fetal rights threaten abortion legislation. If the fetus is granted rights, the door is open to restrict abortion.

[111] "Laci and Conner's Law puts the Abortion Debate in Focus," *The Chicago Tribune*, May 20, 2003, http://articles.chicagotribune.com/2003-05-20/news/0305200385_1_laci-peterson-unborn-victims-abortion-debate (accessed March 10, 2013). "Abortion-rights groups are alarmed that Congress might, for the first time, recognize a fetus as a potential victim independent of the expectant mother." Ibid., Gallagher, "What's Wrong with Fetal Rights?" "While acknowledging the deep emotions that fetuses may evoke for millions of Americans, the

ACLU opposes the creation of theories of fetal rights. (The ACLU) will examine such lawsuits and legislation with a critical eye. If they pose a real threat to reproductive rights, as they often do, then (the ACLU) must intervene and oppose them."

[112] Ibid., Tumuly and Cimons, "Clinton Lifts Restrictions on Abortion: Health: President Ends Ban on Fetal Tissue Research". Ibid., "Fetal Tissue Research," *Wert's Encyclopedia of American Law.*

[113] Ibid., The White House, "Removing Barriers to Responsible Scientific Research Involving Human Stem Cells". Ibid., NIH, "The Promise of Stem Cells".

[114] Guido Heinen, "Humanity: A Matter of Definition," *World Press Review (Volume 51, Number 4)*, April 2004, http://www.worldpress.org/Europe/1842.cfm (accessed March 10, 2013).

[115] Ibid., The White House, "Removing Barriers to Responsible Scientific Research Involving Human Stem Cells". Ibid., Tumuly and Cimons, "Clinton Lifts Restrictions on Abortion: Health: President Ends Ban on Fetal Tissue Research". Ibid., NIH, "The Promise of Stem Cells". Ibid., "Fetal Tissue Research," *Wert's Encyclopedia of American Law.*

[116] Ibid., The White House, "Removing Barriers to Responsible Scientific Research Involving Human Stem Cells". "The purpose is to remove limitations on scientific inquiry, to expand NIH support for the exploration of human stem cell research, and in so doing to enhance the contribution of America's scientists to important new discoveries and new therapies for the benefit of humankind. The Secretary of Health and Human Services (Secretary), through the Director of NIH, may support and conduct responsible, scientifically worthy human stem cell research, including human embryonic stem cell research." Ibid., "Fetal Tissue Research," *Wert's Encyclopedia of American Law.* Those who favor fetal tissue research contend that it has already led to significant medical gains and argue that researchers have an ethical duty to relieve suffering and cure diseases; that fetal tissue research contributes greatly to this cause.

[117] Ibid., *Declaration of Independence.* U.S. Constitution, 14th Amendment. In part, "...nor shall any state deprive any person of life...nor deny to any person...equal protection of the laws."

[118] Ibid., Norrgard, "Human Testing, the Eugenics Movement, and IRBs".

[119] "German Legislation: Embryo Research," January 1991, http://www.eshre.eu/ESHRE/English/Guidelines-Legal/Legal-documentation/Germany/Embryo-research/page.aspx/369 (accessed March 9, 2013).

[120] William E. May, *Human Existence, Medicine and Ethics*, (Chicago: Franciscan Herald Press, 1977), 104. Choosing abortion is morally permissible when the life of the mother is at risk. In these cases, the mother intends to carry the child to term, but a medical condition prevents carrying the child to viability. For example, the pregnant woman has cervical cancer or a cancerous uterus. The doctor performs a hysterectomy as the primary medical procedure to save the life of the mother, resulting in the abortion death of the fetus as a secondary, unintended consequence.

[121] "The Dred Scott Decision," *The History Place*, 1996, http://www.historyplace.com/lincoln/dred.htm (accessed January 19, 2013). The Supreme Court

gave this ruling in March of 1857. Overall, the Dred Scott decision had the effect of widening the political and social gap between the North and South, and took the nation closer to the brink of Civil War.

[122] National Committee for a Human Life Amendment, "Human Life Amendment," 2013, http://nchla.org/issues.asp?ID=46 (accessed February 17, 2013).

[123] Ibid.

[124] Ibid.

[125] Martin Luther King, Jr., "I Have a Dream," August 28, 1963, http://www.americanrhetoric.com/speeches/mlkihaveadream.htm (accessed February 18, 2013). Abraham Lincoln, "Gettysburg Address," November 19, 1863, http://www.abrahamlincolnonline.org/lincoln/speeches/gettysburg.htm (accessed February 18, 2013). Ibid., *Declaration of Independence*.

[126] Ibid., *NSS*, 6, 36.

[127] Ibid., *Declaration of Independence*.

[128] Ibid.

[129] Ibid., Nye, *The Future of Power*, 83.

[130] Ibid.